WHAT WE BURY CHANGES THE GROUND

What We Bury
Changes the Ground

Susan Landgraf

TEBOT BACH • HUNTINGTON BEACH • CALIFORNIA • 2017

Cover art: Tony Phuong
Author photo credit: Lisa Nichols
Book design: Gray Dog Press, Spokane, WA

ISBN-10: 1-939678-38-2
ISBN-13: 978-1-939678-38-6
Library of Congress Control Number: 2017944952

A Tebot Bach book
Tebot Bach, Welsh for little teapot, is a Nonprofit Public Benefit
Corporation, which sponsors workshops, forums, lectures, and
publications. Tebot Bach books are distributed by Small Press
Distribution, Armadillo and Ingram.

The Tebot Bach Mission: Advancing literacy, strengthening
community, and transforming life experiences with the power of
poetry through readings, workshops, and publications.
This book is made possible through a grant from The San
Diego Foundation Steven R. and Lera B. Smith Fund at the
recommendation of Lera Smith.

www.tebotbach.org

This book is dedicated to those in my birth family who did
their best to raise me especially my grandmother,
Mary (Tomaskovics) Mogar

&

To the family, including friends, I've been given in my adult life
especially my husband Dick (1935–2010) and my children
Brett Landgraf
Theodore Landgraf
Jennifer Landgraf
and
Lisa Nichols

Contents

I

II

III

IV

V

VI

What We Bury
Changes the Ground

I

we dig up mollusks
and bones, the stories
we're hungry for

What We Bury Changes the Ground

Picture this body dumped where a pond
used to be, one of those new spit-between—
the neighbor developments, picture windows
looking in other windows. Picture a cement truck
pouring concrete over the body because the driver
didn't know. And the people of the house living
with the corpse under their breathing at night,
a corpse lying in its history
of pollywogs and ponds.

Cast in concrete, the body can't hear rain fall
on the roof and woodpeckers setting up a racket.
He can't hear frogs or children who don't come
for tadpoles, because of the fence.
He doesn't complain, *The noise. The noise.*
Can't a guy get a good night's sleep?

Or say it's she who's restless for petals
to fall like silk across her cheek or the three
o'clock sun warm on her breasts, the sting
of blackberry vines and the sweet,
sweet juice staining her tongue. She can't say,
That's good. That's enough.

People above ground don't remember the muck.
They forget living that goes on in the dark: moles
and roots sucking water. They forget the land could,
at any moment, heave. But that body,
that body wanting to feel the lay
of leaves, tickle of hair roots, mites grumbling;
wanting to feel moon pulling
the water, water being an ultimate blessing,
that body's restless.

II

light tried crawling in
cellar windows
and the one door out

Going Out

Mother teased the film
around her toes, up her arch,
heel, body stretched forward,
fingers massaging the creases.

I hitched myself lower
beside the bureau.

She bent to left, inched
the silk to her calf, knee, thigh as if
she had all the time in the world, as if
she didn't want this to end.

I tucked my hands
in my coat pockets.

She stood, pinched a half-inch
of silk into each shiny clasp
dangling from the garter belt, right
leg first, then left, palms pressed
a moment against her thighs,
eyes closed, then stepped
into sling-strapped
black heels, and

layered under cotton
and wool, my skin
goose-bumped,
burned.

The Cemetery

I didn't want to dress in my snow pants and coat, boots, muffler, hat and go outside into the cold Studebaker to pick up my father. He said he was sorry, my mother said, and scooted us up the stairs out of the cellar into the snowy night. I scrunched into my coat. Sharon whimpered, I'm cold. Cry baby, I told her. Shhh, our mother said. Well, it's cold, Linda said, her teeth chattering.

My mother fiddled with the heater knob, bent to see around the flip-flapping wipers. Where are we going? we chorused in the dark car on the snow-covered road. She leaned further into the steering wheel. Where is he? Waiting at the cemetery by the front gate, she said.

I knew dead people couldn't see out of their graves. Maybe they'd gone to heaven, at least some of them, like my grandmother said, and that's how they could do it: watch from their graves even when they were dead, even when they were covered with dirt. Maybe all the dead turned into magicians, like the one I saw make scarves disappear and a rabbit come out of a hat.

Why's he waiting there? Linda asked. Who took him there? Sharon had fallen asleep, her head cocked to the side like her rag doll. How lucky she was little; it was okay to fall asleep when you were only four.

The snow fell harder. The headlights showed flakes like white needles slicing the yellow light beams. We were alone on the road. He was crying, my mother said, when he called.

Why was he waiting by a gate if everyone was dead inside? Why have a fence? Why bury people if they're dead?

A cold blast blew in with the open door. He slammed it shut. I scrunched down into my coat again. I thought about how the sheets in my bed would feel like ice.

Outhouse

Hot, flies buzzing so loud they sounded bigger
than I was. And the smell. Grandma said
it wasn't as bad as I made out. But I tried covering
my nose at the same time I pulled my underpants
down, hitching myself up on the hole
furthest in, me having to go worse
than Linda. She was on the other hole, both of us
wanting to get back to our dolls, the dusty
July afternoon. She said later my scream was soft
sounding and she screamed louder than I did,
my grandfather racing around the corner, how they
had to move the outhouse, him and a neighbor,
and how grandma couldn't help pinching her nose
before she went to the house and pumped water
into the wash tub, stripped me down to nothing
right there in the yard, grandfather and the neighbor
saying, *It sure is a hot day,* swearing as they set
the outhouse back over the two holes, Linda
dancing up and down whispering,
I have to go, Grandma, I have to go.

Visiting the Painesville Dump with Uncle Judy

Smoke bunched like bushes,
rose into grey lids to trap the smell
of garbage, burning rubber, and wood.
I covered my nose.
With the other hand I held my uncle's
thick fingers. He didn't mind having
a girl's name or a nose bigger than Durante's.
He jabbed at a tire, wrench, rusty saw.
      People are crazy what they throw away.

We crunched over the man-made mountain
of peelings and paper, dishes
and baby cribs. Too embarrassed to tell
kids at school I went to the dump
with my uncle on weekends, I still wished
he was my father.
      Dump is a good thing, he said.
      Holds the rats to one part of town.

My aunt sent me to the tub
before disease took hold.
Some nights, me buried under garbage
and Uncle Judy shooshing rats so loud
he couldn't hear them chewing
my toes and throat, he startled me awake
with his rasp-like whisper.
      Want to see what I made
      from that stuff we dragged home?

I followed him into the bulb-lit
basement smelling of sawdust and paint:
blue and white birdhouses,
clothes trees shaped like giraffes,
and a wagon to replace the one my father smashed.

Harvest

My grandfather sat in his cellar with the furnace
and coal, grandma moving upstairs, trains whistling
loss a block away. He was glad he wasn't headed
    back to the old country, to his father's
    fields. Here he had his onions and plums, corn
    and grapes pressed in September, garlic braided
    before winter, hung to dry.
           He said this country moved too fast:
    Cleveland in an hour, Hungary a day. The sky
was intended for starlings and crows.
    But habit was the best hope he had and the earth
    growing what he asked, my grandmother knowing him
    enough after fifty years not to; it was good,
           he said, she had her Jesus.
He had his Green River Whiskey and grandchildren
    who brought the only surprises. We asked
    for ice cream, coins, and what he had left
    in his lunch pail. He patted a nickel
    in our palms. He told us the dirt under his nails
were filings from the moon.

After the Soaps

Did you want love? I asked
    my grandmother, each week day watching
Search For Tomorrow, All My Children,
The Guiding Light, their black
    and white windows on real-as-life
    hospitals, bars, bedrooms where some
kisses went on as if people didn't
have to breathe, and there was always
a beginning, a middle, an end.
Grandma sat with her shoes off and the reek
of bunions and callouses inside
her heavy stockings filled the room.
    Did you want love? I asked again.
She put her shoes on, tied the laces.
Time to start supper.

Sunday Dinner

I didn't think of pigs wallowing
in mud, feces of the pen,
pigs' guts filled with cabbages
and slop. I didn't think of squeals, then
barnyard silence, a dozen feet
wrapped in white paper at the butcher's and double-
knotted with string, grandma's stubby fingers worrying
the package open on the Formica table.
The kitchen burbled with pots of boiling things.
In white soup bowls, jelly cooled a light amber
around the feet, waiting for Sunday—crocheted
tablecloth, creamy webs holding her china
and silver. My grandparents' guttural voices
mixed with pinging forks and knives and our slurping
as we sucked jelly out of the feet. *More,*
more, my grandfather urged us eat. Grandma asked,
Did you learn your Bible verse
today? And my sisters and I chorused:
"Give not that which is holy
unto the dogs, neither cast your pearls before swine,
lest they trample them under their feet, and turn
again and rend you."
I didn't think of the pigs.

The Woodshed

I liked the smell of wood stacked like walls inside walls. But there was something else—a metallic smell. When I was brave, I ran in, counted the seconds I stayed with my feet planted in the dirt—five, six seconds before I was out with the bees buzzing my grandmother's roses.

One day I bet myself I could go in and pull the door shut. When the outside latch dropped with a metal click, I stood while my skin crawled up my back. Slivers of light under the door needled the walls.

And there he was with wicked eyes that looked like twin flashlights. The priest had talked about evil. I smelled evil. I heard evil breathing. I knew he was searching for an axe, he was going to lift it up and bring it down, just like Gram killed her chickens. One minute they were pecking for corn, the next they were running around without their heads. She laid them down. She held them with her left hand. She raised the axe with her right. Blood splayed and fell like rain. I remembered Christ dying on the cross, but I wouldn't rise again. I was wetting my pants.

When my grandmother screeched the shed door open, I ran to the rectangle of light and burrowed into her apron.

I'll try to be good, I promised. I will try to be very, very good.

My Grandmother's Stories, Translated

1. The Old Country
I scrunched into myself, leaned against
the clapboard siding. Steam rose off
the cow pies. Even with my hands
over my ears, I heard my mother's screams,
the midwife's insistent "Push. Push." How
could a baby live inside my mother's screams
like that? God was angry. I didn't know why.

2. The Crossing
Vomit and feces, days without baths, so many
bodies huddled into each other, against each other
in the pitch of the ship, a bottle ready to break open
in the Atlantic. A day out, and I couldn't
believe there was land on the other side
of that heaving sea, waves higher than any hill
I'd seen in Osku. In that hold, that substitute
ground, nothing grew but moans and questions.
Even with my eyes closed, my stomach rocked
and I smelled how we all wanted to die down there.

3. The Birth
My body shuddered like a house in a high
wind, shutters loose, banging against my ribs.
This was July and I was alone, this baby
wanting to come too soon. I wanted to be
out staking peas. God napped under a tree.

I wrapped white flannel around her fingers
without nails, legs like chicken legs, and toes
the size of peas picked too early. I nested
her, the size of half a loaf of bread
in a shoe box lined with boiled rags

in the cook stove warming oven. I named
her Rosemary, for strength and endurance.

I dreamed an apron full of tender green
globes and woke to a bird's cry, lifted
my daughter, light as a canary's wish bone,
willed her to hold. I remember God
napping under the tree, how I wanted
to hit him over the head with my hoe.

4.
I told my grandchildren they were
lucky and beautiful but what did they know,
playing with their dolls, chasing leaves
in and out of the clothes flapping on the line.
Rosie's three girls. She told them to be good.
She covered her ears during
thunderstorms just like I had.

5. The Roses
Rose from my garden in the glass bowl
on the kitchen table—
        that rose I cut to give
myself. When I get to the gate, God's
        going to ask about the hoe
and my love for roses.

Wing

Tufts of my mother's hair
marked a trail.
Nights my sisters and I lay rigid
as steel pipes.

Next morning we ate cereal,
mother's housecoat pinned
at the neck. *Shhh,*
she said, *your father's sleeping.*
Shhh, she said, when he was home,
like a locked door,
except when he promised.

Each time we believed.
We believed the neighbor boy
when he begged to see the bird nest
in the alder, when he climbed just to look

shook the nest and laughed
to see them falling—eggs, twigs,
grass, feathers.

Threes

the darling daughters
they've lost their father
and don't know how to find him

could be the tavern at Blackmore
and Highway 99 where he puts
up his dukes and takes the fight

home to the darling daughters
in the house he built of brick and stone
no wolf can blow down

children carrying their arms to shield
the Jane Eyre landscape, noses pinched
against Lake Erie's rotted fish

the wind huffing and puffing
in their landlocked childhoods
the girlchilds afraid of crossing bridges

with Billy alive and well, their maps
lost and they've given up
on flowers, on visiting their grandmother

the wolf still outside the door and no
pie for supper, so they feed
themselves on grim

stories: men adrift in a sieved bowl
and how putting posies to your nose
won't save you from the plague

three darling daughters mastering
hide and seek, trying to find
the three primary light sources

at least the three fates present
at each child's birth to decide her fate
the three dragging their addictions

behind them, searching for sturdy ships
and sensible shoes, for the secrets
of triangles and a realtor

to sell the beautiful house
taunting the happy-ever-after ending
catch me, catch me

The Burned-up Men, Fairport, Ohio

Uncle Judy wore chartreuse specks
on his face and hands, coughed
yellow phlegm into handkerchiefs
disintegrating from the bleach
my aunt used on washdays.
    She soaked his work clothes
in cold water first, *the water sick*
and good for nothing after.
When she licked her lips, she tasted salt.

Three shifts, hundreds of men, the ore
from Australia to liquid to car
bumpers, thirty-seven-and-a-half years
manning a long poker to break
the rings in the kilns, heat holding
the fine powder like dust motes
growing yellow-green trails,
the ditches glowing.
    After the Chromate closed
he tracked obituaries in the morning paper.

Twice a week my aunt sat in a lawn chair
at his grave, complained about arthritis
and the nuclear power plant in Painesville,
how one day she knew
it was going to blow.
    When she got to the cancer
I should have known
when I tasted the salt.

My Father, after Magritte's Pipe Paintings

Ceci n'est pas une pipe.
Yes, this is not a pipe.
This is not my father
who did not send me a pipe, but five

of them with a letter he never mailed.
This is not his carpenter's hand
wrapping the package, writing the address
to a town on the opposite coast, but my aunt

who found the letter and pipes,
tobacco left in two of their bowls;
who said because I was the eldest
I should have them.

And the letter, blue lined, penciled:
how one day I would know what it is like
to love. Twenty years waiting
for a magician or god

to hold fire without scars.
Now I have five pipes and a northeasterly
bearing down. I scrape out old tobacco,
tamp in new. Five times no father

still is no father, and this is not
my father's hand lighting the match,
not my father puffing smoke
into vaporous snake or halo.

Sharon

They laid you in the grave, casket
lowered with ropes, a bank of flowers
on top, red ones, into the pit
two men shoveled just hours
ago. I wanted to fling them,
carnations and roses, over
the hedge, pry the casket open,
pull you out to lie in the clover
and October sun, out of that salmon
colored dress that made your skin
look rotted. I'd carry you down
for the creek's benediction
out from under the pink granite headstone
through the oak-dappled afternoon.

III

draw a map
but keep bread crumbs
in your pocket

The Day After

Star like a red gumball,
my mouth open.

The doe so close
to the highway I could reach.

Moon over the waves,
a yellow road

after the sun set between
two nuclear stacks in Satsop

like Christ with the two thieves.
Dawn: waves falling into shore

like they should, the sun
coloring their breaks

faint as washed blood.
The gulls crying.

October 31st

I fell in the ditch
muddied my tutu.
For a month mother parceled out the candy.

I shivered under a nurse's cape
trusted neighbors not to embed
blades in the apples.

I tried on Superman
believed I could fool death
Into thinking I was someone else.

I saw the humor in cycles:
Christian saints over the Celtic
celebration and bags full of candy.

Houdini perfected "The Vanishing
Elephant" and "Walking Through a Brick Wall."
He wasn't chained or cuffed

the day he died.
But I practice cynicism
the perfect costume.

Finding Curtis Smith's *Ancestral Voices* with Color Illustration by Richard Williams

Axes and picks leach color out of the French sky. There they are, this
family of five, plus assorted others: infant and mammal bones buried
in the limestone, bones from two or three million years back, as if years
were clouds scuttling the sky. Except the man with the axe isn't thinking
of clouds. He isn't thinking how frail life is, only how his back jars with
the swings he takes, axe biting limestone, shocking his arms and feet,
as he clears the way for the bed of the railroad. He isn't thinking they'd
lain there longer than fifty times a hundred fingers and toes and how
lasting bones are, how clouds are passing over their heads the same, them
standing upright once on limestone with their flints. If there had been a
thunderstorm, if the sun had broken through and they'd looked up, they
would have seen the rainbow. They would have bowed or raised their
arms or dropped their mouths for what they couldn't understand.

The man with the axe building a railroad knows more, his arms raised—
but not seeing, under the French sky in 1868, the satellites one day
circling, manmade discs taking their place with the stars, the world not
yet having cell phones and faxes to tell the news, not having a flag to
plant on the moon, the man with the axe not looking at the sky but into
the limestone grave as if they had died yesterday.

Finding My Grandmother's Birth Place, Osku, Hungary

The woman goes grave to grave
under shawl, apron,
babushka on a hot
August afternoon.
Tin watering can
holds her lopsided
among the wilted
daisies, sky ripped
open by jets. Horses
clip-clop the cobblestones,
wagons piled with hay,
air filled with the drone
of bees. She holds dried
leaves swept from the plots,
points to a thatched house,
stoops again. Sun-hot
weeds stir in a poof
of breeze in the ditch
by the graves: Zozsef,
Nagy, Tomaskovics.

After the Oracle at Delphi

Men, hands poised mid-move, deliberate
over chess boards in front of the cafe.
Women sweep out their doorways.

Hundred-degree sun bleaches columns spilled
over the countryside, fields filled with sounds
of cicadas and raspy grasses.

After dark the air smells of olives and heat
and star after star after star falls into a chasm
next to the taverna.

At the Bar a Guy in a Black Robe Explains

See that planet pulse and explode in a light so blinding there had to
be darkness in the beginning. See that magma catapulted by a giant's
hand out of the volcano to bring fire down from the mountains. See
those rocks, mute on the plain in the Andes. Viracocha breathed and
that's when the rocks who were men and women woke. See those stones
holding up the terraces in Pisco and the summer palace at Machu Picchu.
See those gods doing what all gods do, creating arms and legs to wrap
around each other in their images. See those little rocks letting go of their
mothers, rolling down, crashing through windows and the rocks in their
slings, all the other rocks, all the other planets and stars waiting their
turn.

Santorini

Volcanic cones sketch
a dragon's back. Fira clings
to the rim, white exclamations
touching the kind of blue
a hand could get lost in.

After Thera erupted
governments changed, men
dying faster with knives,
slower with envy.

After daily hordes of tourists,
houses and churches hold
the hills with tomatoes, grapes,
and the air
is someone breathing.

In the House of the Silver Wedding

Places light will not go—
clay jars, ovens, bread loaves and fish,
the 25 brothels, dining rooms and grinding mills waiting
for someone to come. It was the deadness
of Pompeii struck Sir Walter Scott.
        Then there are shadows
giving lie to the dead, sun dyeing
a courtyard entrance the kind of bright
I had to shield my eyes against.

My ear to the rut of the road, I don't hear
Mount Vesuvius rumble. Cicadas scratch
the dusty air and grasses flick stone walls.
A chariot is coming with a fast black steed
and a woman who wears midnight blue.
The hem of her gown escapes
the carriage, cutting my cheek like a blade in her rush.
The dinner party waits. Her fish lies
untouched—and the goat, the humans cowered
beneath their beds, crouched in a well, caught
in jewel-box rooms where yellow, turquoise, and red
murals preserve the marriage of Venus and Mars.
The three graces of Dionysus never intervened.
Even Ulysses, who would not listen
to the sirens' song, offered no salvation.
Only Venus in her seashell
might have escaped. When the city wakes
citizens wait, willing to show their facial hairs and agony
in liquid plaster.

I carry grapes, roses and hibiscus from Capri,
          careful not to leave anything
of myself here. Out of death,
I fear the gods
following me home.

Why Some Hungarians Dream Equations and Notes

More musicians and mathematicians
than anywhere else: too many Martians, not enough
spaceships to take them back—the sudden exodus
like a great flock of herons
slipping through a blue lip in the sky.

The gypsy women's skirts unfurl
to red and purple flowers, and the men's voices
reverberate like echoes
in a well. Their stories
flicker around the campfire: how the abandoned

pocketed themselves from the sea and the moon's pull,
whirled to the hum a compass needle makes
in the dark. They used scales as metaphors.
Their long-handled cups held the moon.
They mixed with the natives.

Finding blue bloods now would be hard as going home
without a ship—but a thread holds
the magnetic resonance in their equations,
their songs throbbing
with a blue planetary hum.

IV

scatter mustard seeds—
follow the moon
the celestial hum

Reading the Tarot: The Gypsy Migration Story and Butterflies, Copper

It's in my hands. They want to lift, pick the moon.
It's in the cards wrapped in red silk
embossed with gold flowers so thin light shows in.
It's in the cards, her side of the family out of Slovakia, my grandmother
    said,
trekking from her garden to sink to stove to table.
I was out under the porch building sand castles,
smells of cabbage soup, paprika, strudel
leaking through the screen door. I built roads and rivers.
I drew stars. I drew the seven of hearts with fluttering wings
on Lake Erie's shore.

Three, five, the odd numbers falling out
of the 21 majors, uneven number
again, numerals sparking the dark like fireflies
I caught in a Kerr jar. Little golden chariots. I followed
their light until I let them go.
I could feel the dark in my veins. I tried
not to be afraid.

Women danced on the calendar my grandfather had nailed
to the cellar wall next to the coal bin, one
of the women dancing with her skirt and petticoats
billowing above her naked buttocks, her feet, arms,
face, all of her rising, spinning around ornamented
rhythms I breathed
into a spiral of fiery roses.
A flame, no body.

They were penny moons, silver-coined tambourines
I spanked and jangled in grade school. My wrist snapped
a path out of India to Egypt, listening

to the creaking wheels, wanting to see
some other side. As if the earth
was a coin to flip. Day, night—wheels within wheels.
Sun gone, the woman brought out a globe,
spread the cards and charged to see the other side.
Death, justice with pennies, and a magician
who lived in both worlds, who decided
what was real.

One push on my grandmother's porch glider to Cleveland
and my aunt's corner grocery, oiled floors, sausage
behind the glass case, pickles, garlic. I could take
one licorice stick. Three pushes to Africa, four for China.
At night the train shook my metal bed, sparked
the tracks like hair-thin lightning tongues
a quarter moon away. No matter Christ hung
framed above my bed, head encircled by a thorn crown,
his red heart quivering. I knew what the Queen
of Swords foretold: Enter and leave alone.
She wore a butterfly crown and lace. The train whistled
itself to a ghost, I stopped shaking.

Fortune showed a powerful storm
in the full moon. No one can escape
the swords that fall when it's time. Ice covers the land,
mountains erupt. That's what the card says, she said, the teller
of the cards. No one can escape when it's their time
for misery, the swords blood-shined, the forces like an inferno.
See the red, she said. Forget you're afraid. Remember the garden crowned
with ripe tomatoes and what the road looked like under the moon, shape
    shifting
the clouds, weaving itself through the leafless trees.

Bees buzzed the ripened plums, their juice like resin.
Garden almost spent, my grandmother's kitchen steamed

with the canning, her knife coring, slicing, dicing for the jars.
He'd come once a year across the fields that stretched
every direction, house to house across Hungary, she said, with his pots
and pans clanking like a two-key band in the wagon, came each
year with his grinding wheel to sharpen the knives. He told stories,
she said, people who were good, people dancing with the devil
inside them. He told how his horse knew the road without stars or moon.
How the road was a river leading to its source,
to the telling of life in the faces of the cards. The Two of Pentacles
shaped an eight. Two snakes, one shedding its skin at the right time,
stars dying, hens birthing eggs for breakfast and for chicks
into hens into the Sunday dinner pot. Grandma used the axe,
then her knife like a sixth finger on her right hand for the rest.

I had to trust the driver who spoke no English to take me
to Osku, where the photograph from the old country
showed a family standing in the doorway, dark dresses,
baby with bonnet tied tight under her chin. They had one cow,
a few geese; they had so little, grandmother said, believing
in good, filling the boxes with donated hats, coats, and boxes of Kraft
macaroni and cheese. She'd lived with newspapers in her shoes
to outlast the cold winds that swept the fields
on her walk to school. An orange at Christmas, if they were lucky,
like a miracle. Each slice a sweet pocket moon in the hoarfrost of winter.
This new country had bins and bins of oranges all year, so
who needed roads paved with gold, she said.

Geese honked and my driver pointed, made hand gestures
with a pretend fork from steering wheel to mouth.
Inside the cave, electric bulbs dangled over the scratched tables,
mismatched chairs, blue and white flowered china,
heavy forks and knives, the cave filled
with its molten heat and secret fissures, a womb out of the chaos
of lightning, breathing the breath of itself
and the smells of potato soup, chicken paprikash, and strudel.

My stomach glowed with the memory of it.
Her kitchen. My grandmother, a four-foot-eight
queen of abundance. The memory of it, caves out of the beginning
of some birth, some time,
somewhere long back.

In a coffee house in Budapest, the smudged-faced
girl sidled up to our table and put out her palm,
dirt-caked, fingernails bitten.
Her eyes glinted above her childlike smile. The waitress
shooed her away—but not before I put my uneaten pastry in her hand,
not before she looked down and spat,
before she disappeared like a thin penny
through the door.

In the town of Papa, relatives on my grandfather's side
said, eat, eat. The table bloomed with plates and dishes of food.
Drink the slivorice, the plum brandy, in one gulp for good luck,
for coming across the great ocean, drink, it is our habit.
Eat more goulash, more poppy seed horns. See
how your grandfather looks in this picture and you a baby
and your grandmother sent us pictures and how the whole village knew
when the boxes came and how we stood around
like it was an altar.

Drink and your grandfather's brother's grandson will continue
to translate. Look how we kept those years
and your grandfather who rode the great sea.
Those boxes your grandmother mailed smelled like America.
We wore the clothes, ate the food and we kept the pictures.
They shuffled the stack of black and white photographs
that showed part of the story. America, America,
the old man of the family whispered. America, he breathed.
Where we know now your roads are paved with rocks, his son
added, like our roads. But here you are, like a wish,

44

and your grandfather knows you have come.
So drink. Drink.

I studied The Fool who is without malice. He wore
a pouch filled with memories of the world.
He traveled over mountains under clear light.
He held a wand with the head that looks
backward to show past and present. He walked
without desire. So simple. I was the Copper Woman
dancing in my ancestors' fields of corn and sunflowers.
Butterflies circled their heads. I was the ore,
the conductor of the glider swing to Cape Town,
Leningrad, Beijing, and Osku, still sitting
in the maple tree in my grandmother's yard
hidden on a branch among the large leaves humming
a little, waiting for a prince, for the next train,
my tongue clicking the clackety clack
of the wheels and making wishes.
Two licorice sticks next time. I was
Copper Woman fluttering and sparking
at the same time, my fingers snapping
the ornamented rhythms, mapping
the story, making me a funnel
of light on the river.

V

belly to the ground
I am snake, my old skin
behind me

With Its Ring Like A Bracelet

Last time I backed down the rickety
cellar stairs, spiders had spun a thousand lines
between the beams. A giant from my dreams
still lived under the boards grandfather laid
over wet clay. Now I watch each day going
to winter fast. I've grown no orchards,
kept no jars, let the art of steam and stains
die with grandmother.

But I can't leave it alone—whether I never
went back down for fear of the giant
or reverence for what is bright.
I believe in reaping, storing when it's time,
shelves sagging over the years
of cherries, peaches, and plums,
fruit smooth-fleshed in sweet syrup
like the ones in the cellar
under my grandmother's kitchen.

. . . I slide my hand through the trap
door ring, suck in my breath
before the musty odor, step
down.

Of Arachnids, Myriapods, and Insects I Know This:

Segments unified under a horny
exoskeleton, these arthropods
know it's too late for butterflies.
In this evolution they're stuck,
remarkably, with what they've got:
legs and a history of their ground.
After the soil has acquiesced
to being turned by the spade,
after the bulbs have been planted,
ground tamped, worms wriggle
up, spiders sash shay over the dirt clods,
and my fingers, segmented, too,
try to get a feel of the land
in which I do not,
intimately, live.

Potato Eyes

They push without legs, like cocoons
the color of maggots inveigling
their way past pill bugs, worms,
antennae reaching for the feel
of rain, not just wetness but for
the music of it, by now their eyes
opened, unfurling. They lie
like a memory, waiting for the spade.
They keep their nightshade
family to themselves, pockets growing
among the soil and millipedes, stones
singing their own stories of kingdoms
and uprisings, the potato eaters, miners
and stone masons, all of them knowing
        by the sweat of their brows.

Spiders

See, in that dark basement
I learned, like potato eyes,
to sprout. I kept to corners.
I learned scrutiny without calling
attention to myself, lids
drooping for camouflage.

I learned how Persephone
must have felt, and roots.
They must always go down.
They must feel out opposition:
rocks, foundations, pipes.

It took time, then, adjusting
to air without mold.
To moonlight. The spiders
remind me, as I lay me down
without night lights: I let
them have the run of my house.

Aristotle Called Them the Intestines of the Earth

Once I heard an earthworm talk. My sisters chased me with a can full and I heard them tracking my shoulders, my arms, my neck, worms without mothers and fathers to teach them, worms taking over the world. One of them urged, *Get her. Get her.*

Later I learned they have lips; they have an esophagus, gizzard and digestion; they eat the world: chickory, aspen and ash leaves, corpses, bark. They eat and they shit seven to eighteen tons, enough to keep the world from being stone, dead as the moon. I watched their flexibility, their tubular bodies expanding and contracting, moving more remarkably than humans, more eloquently than any politician or poet. I listen.

But the world is growing office buildings and parking lots. And over the noise, the bulldozers, the drills, the trucks, over the noise, it's hard to hear what I think.

Between Worlds

"When the forest dies, its children die."

Frog song. Crickets. And dragonflies darning
the air. Three-hundred and fifty million years laying
their eggs in the pond stalks or mating mid-
flight, their primitive wings deftly beating, their basketlike
legs scooping prey. This is the garden of nettles
and horsetails, of toadstools and bulging
roots, of quicksand and leeches. And there are the nymphs
out of the water into the air. Three-hundred and fifty
million years of transformation, on the twenty-first day
before their death: shimmering dragons
whirring the lances of light, the forest quickening
to day and its people gathering
peach-palm fruit, mushrooms, fern fronds.

Fungi

Undercover agents
they eat the world
sprays of spores
thousands bursting
from the undersides
of their umbrellas
falling like rain.
In any forest
they know how to survive.

The Reservation at First Beach, La Push

This is the day after the great hatching
males and females coming out
of thin slits in a wooden gallery of wingless
soldiers, workers, nymphs

Earharts and Lindberghs sheathed in wings
longer than their bodies, looking clumsy
but flying high as 19,000 feet
living in the warmth, dying in the sunlight

emerging at sunset and mating before
board feet or the Ortho man were born, hundreds
slipping out of the log, flying
a gauzed sky

but one rust-red grub transversing
the silvered beach log, a soldier
in the dusk before Venus, before the moon sets
on the day after the great hatching.

Lesson of the Order "Lepidoptera"

glowing egg-
shell blue
translucent
pupa   hanging
from a twig

in twelve days
a winged' adult
10 million years
of history
        fluttering
over the four o'clocks
and daisies

transparent wings
colored by scales
        sail-setting
of specialized muscles
delicately

their limbs being
part of their back
        flying
during the day
taste receptors
in their front legs

stained glass
windows
        sucking
nectar
        flaunting
brilliance

Hitler Might Come Again, Disguised. Not the Gardener.

His knees print
the ground,
his hands without gloves
patting the soil
like musical notes
around the delphiniums.
People walk by.
He is studying the color
of day lily leaves
and budding forsythia.
A man and woman
argue about understanding.
He is intent
on cutting back
pampas grass
and rose bushes,
digging out
the dead magnolia,
loading limbs
into a wheelbarrow,
spading the hole
over and over itself
under the rain.
He divides the iris.
He doesn't wear a hat.
The rain
is smoothing out
his hand
and knee prints.

Amphibiously

Come January, they will be waiting
in their living tombs
of mud. Fast-handed kids,

with no fear of murky caches,
can catch them—a trace
of our primordial climb.

Cold-blooded, one frog made
this audacious deal
with a princess. She couldn't take

him for what he was—not a snowy
egret with undulating neck
or the mighty, mythical salmon

thrashing upstream to his death.
Just frogs, with fast tongues
and catapults unexpected

from such dull lumps, each spring
their symphony of sexual longing
a surprise.

Land of Alkali and Chromate

Erie with its dead fish in the '50s, the Cuyahoga River burned. Air filled
with chartreuse particles and the earth wore a witch's lip around ponds of
sulfur, salt, a burbling grey soup waiting for my father to fall into.

He'd grabbed at the slippery sides in the dark, muck sucking his shoes
off. When he finally crawled out, his clothes were set like concrete. The
doctor said, *Being drunk likely saved him.*

Today the river's clean. Erie's got herons and fish.
Diamond's been turned into high-ceilinged apartments
and the Chromate's been razed by men in protective clothing. The land
lies under new grass, fenced.

It will take a hundred years for the ground to grow clean.
Across the railroad tracks, weeds grow around the headstones.

Sacramental

1.
Around the brick and stone house
my father built, daffodils sprouted
in unexpected clumps. Nothing left
but a photo, dark eyes like mine
squinted in the sun, his legs dangling
from the tailgate of a Chevy truck.

2.
I cradle brown paper-wrapped daffodils
and tulips from the old woman
at the public market, her eyes ringed
like tern tracks. Like my grandmother
who grew tulips with the garlic,
hydrangeas, rhubarb and compost.
She troweled, fertilized, mulched, and flashed
her watering can like a tin sun,
her hat an upside-down bird bath.
She shadowed under her layers of apron over
her dress over camisoles and petticoats
bleached the color of cumulus. She got down
every night by the side of her bed to pray
to her Jesus and followed the weather.

3.
Her vase is a blue window,
water clear as a church bell pealing around
a forest of stems—cups full
of sun and small red fists
reaching up.

4.
A train whistle rings the valley—
most tracks torn up, trains like the buffalo,
the land turning like a fractured mind
to deserts
with only one savior—
rain, sweet rain falling
falling sweet.

5.
After the vase slips out of my hands,
I kneel in the puddle of blue shards, knowing
the Garden of Gethsemane at the Mount of Olives
is not my garden, knowing some
of the olive trees are among the oldest known,
knowing why I can't reinvent Babylon's gardens,
but why I need flowers, why
I must build my own garden.

Ordering the World

I go to Babylon's Hanging Gardens, find
them in Nineveh; they might have been
subterranean—and why not? Here is where
Saddam Hussein's army built its base
and where the fighting goes on.
Perhaps, under the talk of villagers, the stones and water
remember their glory and confess they're glad
not to be in the valley of bullets.

I walk the great palace garden paths
at Pasargadae where cypress, pomegranate, cherry,
lilies and roses bloomed; conversations in the two
pavilions fall like leaves. After Alexander
the Great destroyed Persepolis, he visited the tomb
of Cyrus the Great. There he lay—Cyrus who'd founded
the empire of the Persians, Cyrus who asked
for "this little earth that covers my body."

I find Tenochtitlan's floating garden
with its junipers and cocoa, and the axolotl
from the Aztec empire, incarnation of the god Xolotl,
brother of Quetzalcoatl. The amphibian that can
regenerate its limbs and other body parts still lives.
Montezuma could not. Even Cortez could not,
and the canals are drying up. Where
will the migratory birds go?

I search the Valley of the Yellow River
and Suzhou for coy, bamboo, smoke that follows the dragons,
and water lilies large as palace tables. Garden after garden—
Lake of the Supreme Essence, Garden of the Majestic Clear Lake,
and the Dunes of Sand. Zhou and his friends and concubines
drifted in their boats, eating the skewers of roasted meat from the trees,

drinking wine from the pool lined with polished stones.
Zhou said, *Eat. Drink. Let the peasants*
fill their rice bowls with what they can find.

Gardens grow out of what was desolation.
In my grandmother's garden, sunflowers chorused;
roses visited with tiger lilies, hollyhocks,
hydrangeas, and cosmos. Four o'clocks told
the closing hours. Winter always came too soon,
my grandmother said—maple leaves turned skeletal,
flower heads shriveled, stems slimy and slinky
across the ground. She never tried to save them.

I study climate, phosphorous, nitrogen, and seasons,
carry rocks and build walls for planting beds—
replicate gardens from Mesopotamia, Mexico,
China. I water, fertilize, praise each hyacinth,
camellia bloom, nasturtium, aster, and marigold.

I watch two slugs copulate in the steady August rain
on one of the walls I built next to the roses,
slugs eating, eating, eating my marigolds.
I watch their white globulin sacs throb between them.
I pour on the salt.
    I dig. Cut. Kill
for the good of my garden.

VI

hung from the eaves
bleached bones
whittle the wind

Why Jules Verne Wanted to Find the Center of the Earth

                              At the edge
of a marsh, those mired places
with detached clumps of sedge
and life under the scum, hear the muck
sucking to connect ankle bones
and gastropods.
    Inland, marble markers
lean with the ages in the cemeteries
of Kent and Cleveland.

On the coast the beach wears the stunted
pilings of a pier, leftovers from the era
of sporty gentlemen and ladies
with their parasols against the sun
                    before the tsunami hit.
Tonight beachcombers will feed log
after log into a conflagration, a brief
                    illumination.

What an act it is, daily, to rise,
to put on one shoe after the other,
bras, sarongs, crutches and briefcases,
                to walk the land
                waiting to take us back.

Thanks To . . .

I know I will forget some people I should thank for this book. The list is long and I am grateful for the friends, fellow writers, teachers and residencies that have given me friendship and support.

Thank you:
Centrum, Hedgebrook, Ragdale, Soapstone, Whiteley, and Willard R. Espy for residencies where I began or reworked many of these poems.

John Davis, Sharon Hashimoto, Bob McNamara, Arlene Naganawa, Michael Spence, Ann Spiers, and John Willson—my Decasyllable buddies. Claudia Bach, Janet Olson Baker, Hattie Cannon, Catalina Cantu, Caroline Cumming, Kristina Danalchick, Sharon Goldberg, Netter Hansen, Susan Jostrom, David Messerschmidt, Neil Mathison, James Stark, Vlado Vulovic—and especially Karen Lorene who started the Tuesday Supergroup and has kept it going these many years.

Kim Addonizio, Kelli Agodon, Nelson Bentley, Robert Bly, Michele Bombardier, Carolyn and Ken Brettmann, Dianne Butler, Carolyn Forche, Sam Green, Adriane Hartness, Jordan Hartt, Terrance Hayes, Richard Hugo, Lynn and Al Hutteball, Charles Johnson, Mifanwy Kaiser, Gayle Kaune, Dana Levin, Sam Ligon, Gary Copeland Lilley, Marilyn Mahoney, Frances McCue, Colleen McElroy, Jim Mitsui, Ed Morris, Bonnie Nelson, Takami Nieda, Susan Rich, Marjorie Rommel, Lois Rosen, Terryl Ross, Julianne Seeman, Bill Smull, William Stafford, David Wagoner, Diane Westergaard.

And last but not least, Lonny Kaneko, my teacher, friend, and former colleague who required that I write a poem in his class even though I hated poetry (way back then) and Bill Ransom, who first introduced me to Centrum at Fort Worden and the amazing world of fellow poets and writers.

About the Author

A writer and photographer, Susan Landgraf has published more than 400 poems, essays, and articles in more than 150 journals, magazines, and newspapers. Most recently her poems have appeared, or are forthcoming, in *Prairie Schooner, Poet Lore, Nimrod, The Bellingham Review, Kestrel, Margie*, and *The Sow's Ear*. Her chapbook *Other Voices* was published by Finishing Line Press, and a textbook, *Student Reflection Journal for Student Success*, was published by Prentice Hall.

Landgraf has given more than 150 writing workshops ranging from Centrum and the Pacific Northwest Writers Conference to Antioch International, Oxford, England, the Washington State Community College Mathematics Conference, and the Walla Walla State Prison. A book of writing exercises is due out in 2018 from Two Sylvias Press.

Honors include two Pushcart Prize nominations; Pablo Neruda, Society of Humanistic Anthropology, and Academy of American Poets awards; a Jack Straw Productions grant; Centrum, Hedgebrook, Ragdale, Soapstone, Whiteley, and Willard R. Espy residencies, and a Theodore Morrison scholarship at Bread Loaf.

Landgraf taught at Shanghai Jiao Tong University in China in 2002, 2008, 2010 and 2012 through an exchange program with Highline College, where she taught writing, journalism, media, literature, Diversity and Globalism, and college studies classes for 27 years.

About the Cover Artist

Tony Phuong is an artist and graphic designer.

"As a child, I just love to draw more than anything else so in my high school years I started to take some courses from a private art school and taught myself some other painting techniques.

I took refuge at the Thailand refugee camp when the ration was not provided for 3 years because my family was undocumented refugees at the time. Using these skills was the only way that I could create some income to support my family of six (my parents and three other siblings).

Whether work on the art project or graphic design put smile on me."

Acknowledgments

Grateful acknowledgement is given to the following journals that published these poems or earlier versions of them:

Albatross #8: Of Arachnids, Myriapods, and Insects I Know This
American Indian Culture and Research Journal: The Reservation at
　　First Beach, LaPush
Crab Creek Review: The Day After
Crowdancing: Visiting the Painesville Dump with Uncle Judy
Finishing Line Press: "Other Voices" - Potato Eyes
Kaleidoscope: The Burned-up Men, Fairport, Ohio
Least Loved Beasts: Spiders
Nimrod: Amphibiously; Aristotle Called Them the Intestines of
　　the Earth; Between Worlds; Finding Curtis Smith's *Ancestral*
　　Voices with Color Illustration by Richard Williams; My Father
　　After Magritte's Pipe Paintings; Reading the Tarot: the Gypsy
　　Migration Story and Butterflies, Copper; Threes; What We Bury
　　Changes the ground
Poet Lore: Going Out; October 31st
Poetry Repairs: Hitler Might Come Again, Disguised. Not the
　　Gardener.
Pontoon: Sharon; Land of Alkali and Chromate
South Florida Review: With Its Ring Like A Bracelet
Spoon River Review: Wing
The Green Lantern Literary Review: Outhouse
The Laurel Review: Why Jules Verne Wanted to Find the Center of the
　　Earth
The Sow's Ear: Why Some Hungarians Dream Equations and Notes
The Written Arts: In the House of the Silver Wedding
Whole Notes: Lesson of the Order "Lepidoptera"

TEBOT BACH
A 501 (c) (3) Literary Arts Education Non Profit

THE TEBOT BACH MISSION: advancing literacy, strengthening
community, and transforming life experiences with the power of poetry
through readings, workshops, and publications.

THE TEBOT BACH PROGRAMS
1. A poetry reading and writing workshop series for venues such as homeless
shelters, battered women's shelters, nursing homes, senior citizen daycare
centers, Veterans organizations, hospitals, AIDS hospices, correctional
facilities which serve under-represented populations. Participating poets
include: John Balaban, Brendan Constantine, Megan Doherty, Richard Jones,
Dorianne Laux, M.L. Leibler, Laurence Lieberman, Carol Moldaw, Patricia
Smith, Arthur Sze, Carine Topal, Cecilia Woloch.

2. A poetry reading and writing workshop series for the community Southern
California at large, and for schools K-University. The workshops feature
local, national, and international teaching poets; David St. John, Charles
Webb, Wanda Coleman, Amy Gerstler, Patricia Smith, Holly Prado, Dorothy
Lux, Rebecca Seiferle, Suzanne Lummis, Michael Datcher, B.H. Fairchild,
Cecilia Woloch, Chris Abani, Laurel Ann Bogen, Sam Hamill, David Lehman,
Christopher Buckley, Mark Doty.

3. A publishing component to give local, national, and international poets a
venue for publishing and distribution.

Tebot Bach
Box 7887
Huntington Beach, CA 92615-7887
714-968-0905
www.tebotbach.org